History Of Russia For Kids

A History Series

Children Explore Histories Of The World Edition

Speedy Publishing LLC
40 E. Main St. #1156
Newark, DE 19711
www.speedypublishing.com

The early history of **Russia**, like those of many countries, is one of migrating peoples and ancient kingdoms.

Early Russia was not exactly "Russia," but a collection of cities that gradually coalesced into an empire.

Tradition says the Viking Rurik came to Russia in C.E. 862 and founded the first Russian dynasty in Novgorod.

Viking tribes from Scandinavia moved southward into European Russia, tracing a path along the main waterway connecting the Baltic and Black Seas.

The various tribes were united by the spread of Christianity in the 10th and 11th centuries; Vladimir the Saint was converted in 988.

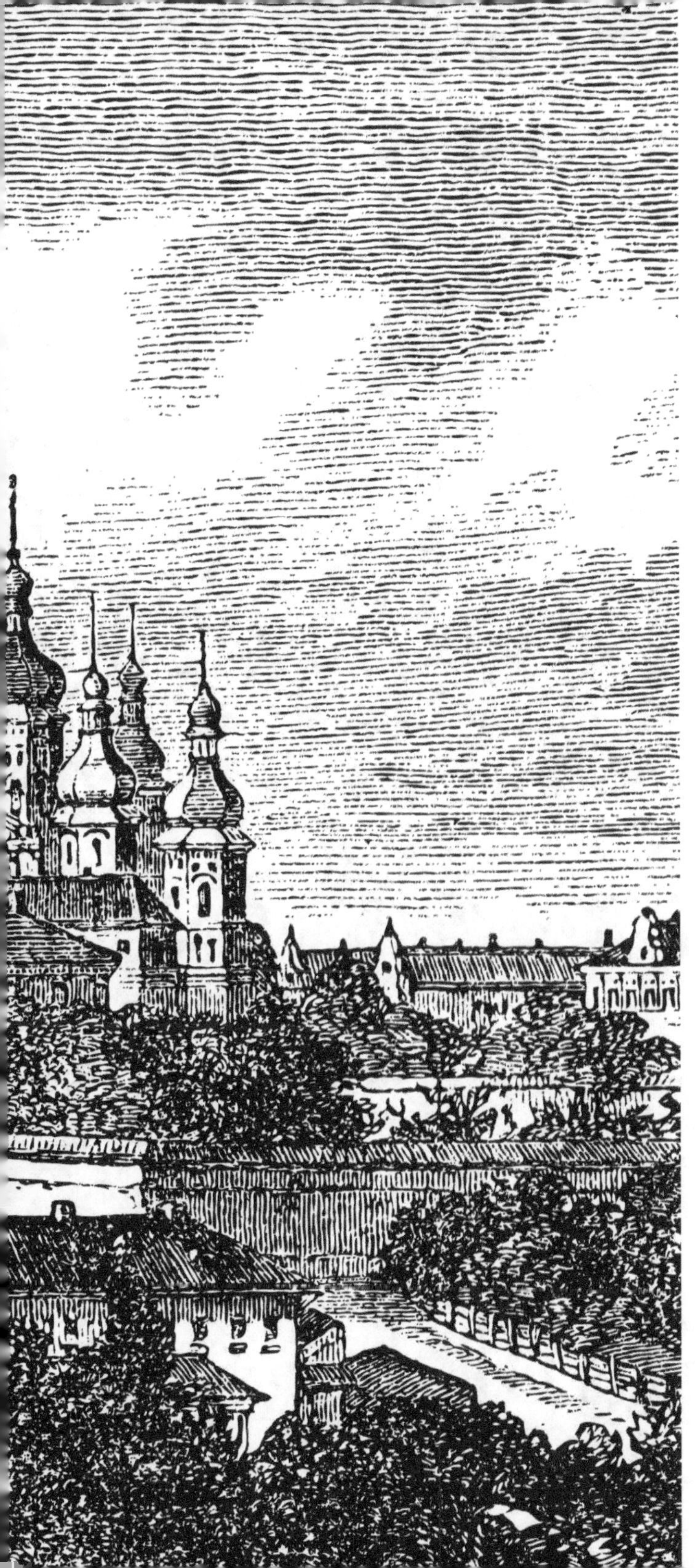

In 1240, Kiev was destroyed by the Mongols, and the Russian territory was split into numerous smaller dukedoms.

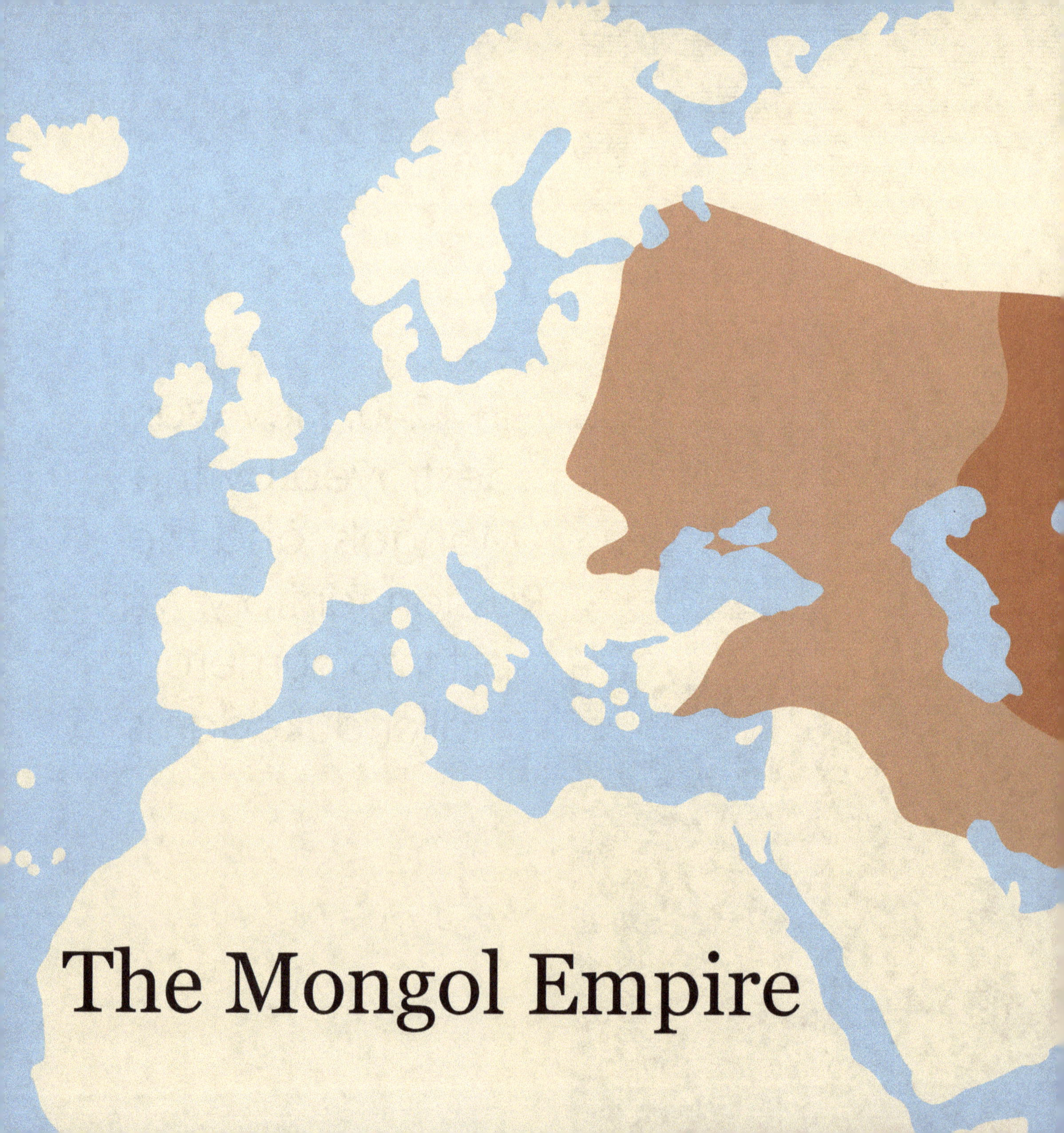

The Mongol Empire

The Mongol
Empire stretched
across the Asian
continent and
Russia was
put under the
suzerainty of the
Khanate of the
Golden Horde.

During the reign of Alexander I (1801-25), Napoleon's attempt to invade Russia was unsuccessful and his troops defeated in 1812, and new territory was gained, including Finland (1809) and Bessarabia (1812).

In the Decembrist
revolt in 1825, a
group of young,
reformist military
officers attempted
to force the
adoption of a
constitutional
monarchy in Russia
by preventing
the accession
of Nicholas I.

The humiliating Treaty of Brest-Litovsk (March 3, 1918) concluded the war with Germany, but a brutal civil war and foreign intervention delayed Communist control of all Russia until 1920.

A brief war
with Poland in
1920 resulted in
Russian defeat.
Emergence of
the U.S.S.R.

ФІНАНСОВУ БАЗУ
БУДОВІ СОЦІАЛІЗМУ
ПЕРЕХІДНИЙ ПРАПОР
...АЙ ГАЗЕТИ «КОЛГОСПНИК
КИЇВЩ...

The Soviet-German collaboration ended abruptly with a lightning attack by Hitler on June 22, 1941, which seized 500,000 square miles of Russian territory.

FUN RUSSIA FACTS

SUECIA
Karlstad
Estocolmo
Goteborg
MAR
Helsinki
Tallin
ESTONIA
LETONIA
Riga
LITUANIA
Vilna
Kaliningrado
POLONIA
Lodz
Varsovia
Wroclaw
Cracovia
Praga
CHEQUIA
ESLOVAQUIA
Bratislava
Budapest
Viena
AUSTRIA
RUMANIA
Berlin
ALEMANIA
Colonia
Frankfurt
Munich
mburgo
PRAGA
jue
CA
Lago
Ladoga
San Petersbu
Yar
Mos
Minsk
BIELORRUSIA
Gorne
UCRANIA
Kiev
MOLDAVIA
Kishi
Od

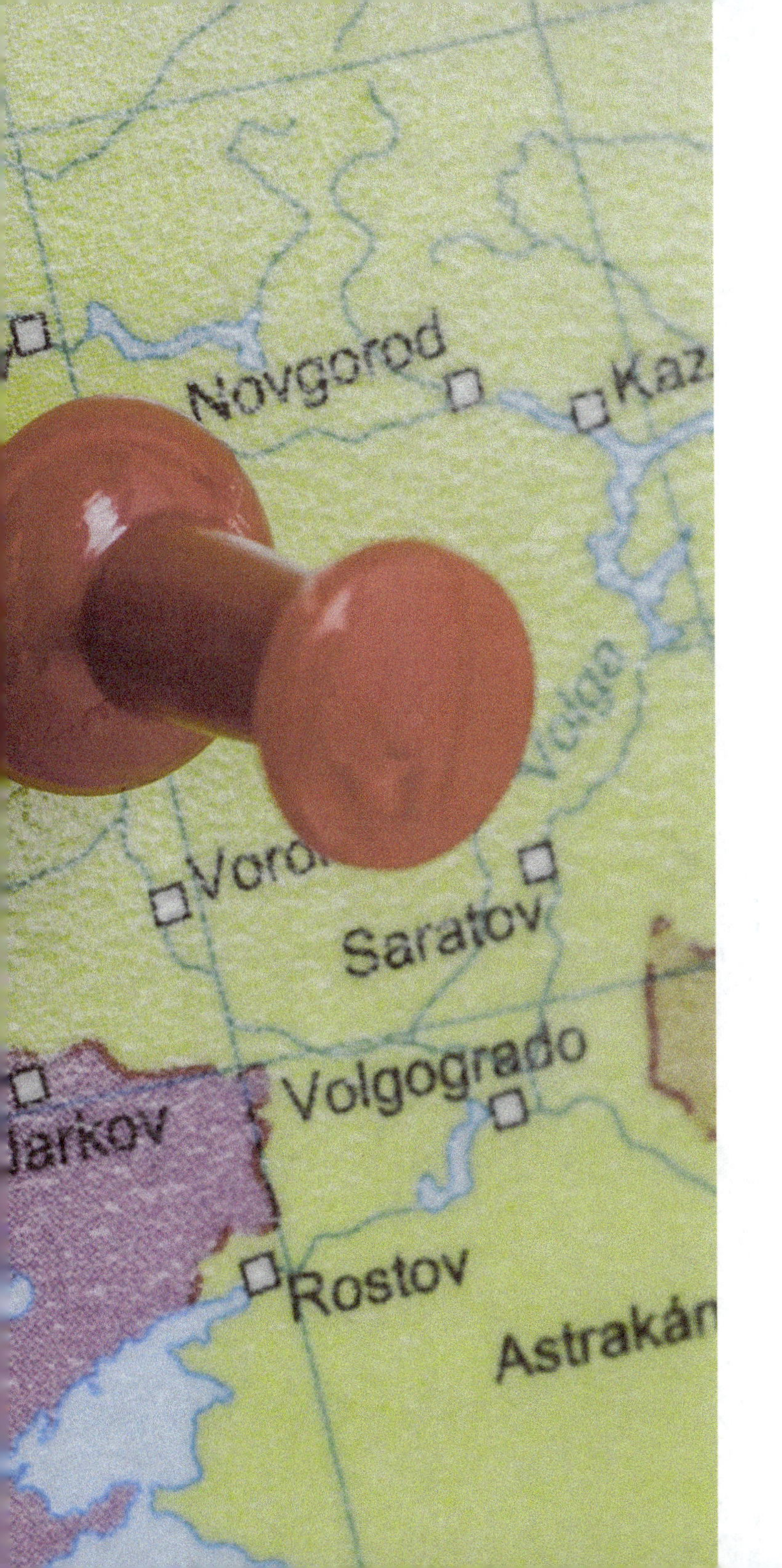

The official name for Russia is the Russian Federation.

Russia has the world's largest area of forests.

HRY XXII. OLYMPIÁDY
MOSKVA 1980
STRNAD 1980 · J. S - M. O

Moscow hosted the 1980 Summer Olympic Games.

The world's
first satellite,
named Sputnik,
was launched
by the Soviet
Union in 1957.

In terms of land area, Russia is the largest country in the world.

The **Russian History** is very rich, research and learn more!

Visit

BABY PROFESSOR
EDUCATION KIDS

www.BabyProfessorBooks.com
to download Free Baby Professor eBooks
and view our catalog of new and exciting
Children's Books

www.ingramcontent.com/pod-product-compliance
Lightning Source LLC
Chambersburg PA
CBHW080817120726
48001CB00009B/2921